Palestine Wail

Poems by
Yahia Lababidi

Daraja Press

Published by
Daraja Press
https://darajapress.com

© 2024 Yahia Lababidi

Cover art: *Symbol of Hope* by Sliman Mansour

Library and Archives Canada Cataloguing in Publication

Title: Palestine wail / Yahia Lababidi.
Names: Lababidi, Yahia, author
Description: Poems. | Includes bibliographical references.
Identifiers: Canadiana 20240417410 | ISBN 9781998309115 (softcover)
Classification: LCC PS3612.A247 P35 2024 | DDC 811/.6—dc23

So many of us are wailing with Yahia Lababidi, who is not afraid to call out truth in the midst of catastrophe, to question heartless power, to embrace so-called conundrums and 'others' who didn't have to be, to grieve for the children who didn't deserve any of this nightmare, and to offer revelations:

> *Radical love understands*
> *#freethehostages means*
> *all Palestinians living*
> *under an inhumane occupation*

Thank you, Yahia, for your passionate care.

— **Naomi Shihab Nye**, author of *Everything Comes Next: Collected and New Poems*

In a time of livestreamed genocide, we the distant witnesses no longer have the luxury of narrated distance. The poet no longer bears witness but attempts to bear the unbearable, to cry out against the systematic destruction of a people. Renowned aphorist Yahia Lababidi's Palestine Wail writes alongside a catastrophe beyond words, trying to shelter in words what remains of our humanity. To be a Minister of Loneliness and Lightkeeper, tending to the light.

— **Philip Metres**, author of *Fugitive/Refuge*

These are necessary and truthful poems. Yahia Lababidi powerfully illuminates this heartbreaking time and terrible season in the history of our world. This book, like a lantern in darkness, brings to light the truth of lives we must learn to honor and remember.

— **James Crews**, author of *Unlocking the Heart: Writing for Mindfulness, Creativity, and Self-Compassion*

In gratitude for those who, with fire in their bones, and a quaking of spirit, are praying and pulsing words that might hold us, contain us, and suffer with us in our hope and solidarity and belief that as Palestine Wails, walls will fall, and the people of the beautiful land will find a different freedom, founded on love and justice, where Yahia Lababidi shows us, hope can keep a secret.

— **Alison Phipps**, UNESCO Chair, Refugee Integration through Languages and Arts

What is astonishing to me about Yahia Lababidi's *Palestine Wail* is not the tenderness and restraint with which he holds a passion of grief and love, or the spare precision with which he names terrible crimes. These I love. What makes me weep with the revelation of kinship is his unwavering allegiance to our shared humanity, his compassion for the wounds that drive cruelty, his ability to envision the world we long to create, far beyond the cramped spaces in which despair imprisons imagination.

— **Aurora Levins Morales**, author of *Rimonim: Ritual Poems of Jewish Liberation*

Yahia Lababidi's *Palestine Wail* is a brave witness to hope in times of war with all its violent savagery. His poems face the horrors of a systemic killing machine, and while he names the trauma inflicted on the Palestinian people he yet dares to believe—and to help us join him in seeing—that "hope can keep a secret."

He reminds us that "[a]part from unceasing prayer, / eloquence takes the form / of tears or kindness and solidarity." And he refuses silence in the face of the unconscionable specter of an unfolding genocide. Across the arc of this collection, Yahia leads us, with the mind of a prophet and the heart of a mystic, from outrage and effrontery toward the verge of solidarity.

His *Wail* reminds us that "[i]f each of us houses the Divine, / then to take another's life / is to murder a piece of G_d." We need reminders like these so that we do not forget that "we belong to each other." We need poems like these that steer us toward that "far shore" he writes of, where if anywhere children—Palestinian and Israeli and the rest— might still learn "to make a wish" for peace.

— **Rev. Mark S. Burrows, PhD**, poet, scholar, and translator, coauthor of *Meister Eckhart's Book of Darkness and Light* and *You Are the Future: Living the Questions with Rainer Maria Rilke*

*This book is dedicated to the memory
of my beloved grandmother,*
Rabiha Dajani.
*Forced to flee her ancestral home in Palestine
at gunpoint nearly 80 years ago, she went on to become
a remarkable educator, activist, and social worker.*

Contents

Introduction: Wounds as Peepholes.................................... xi
Poems
    I: Unbearable Casualties... 1
    II: Lingering at the Threshold 37
    III: On a Far Shore... 67
Afterword: Poetry of Resistance and Resilience................. 89
Acknowledgements.. 97
About the Poet.. 98

Every beautiful poem is an act of resistance.
— Mahmoud Darwish

Poetry fettered, fetters the human race.
— William Blake

Activism is my rent for living on the planet.
— Alice Walker

While in the midst of horror / we fed on beauty –
and that, / my love, is what sustained us.
— Rita Dove

Oh speak, poet, what do you do?
—I praise.
But the monstrosities and the murderous days,
how do you endure them, how do you take them?
—I praise.
— Rainer Maria Rilke

Introduction: Wounds as Peepholes

"Damaged people are dangerous; they know they can survive." That line, from a movie adaption of *Damage* by Josephine Hart, affected me deeply the first time I heard it as a young man. In context, it was delivered as a perverse badge of courage. It also served as a cautionary tale or warning. What happens when our hearts break?

We can live like a hardened scab, impervious to the mighty winds that shake the mutilated world around us, or become more like an open wound, sensitive to the slightest breeze of suffering or injustice we encounter. I believe most of us try both ways and oscillate between one and the other. "The opposite of love is not hate but indifference." This aphorism was coined by Holocaust survivor, Elie Wiesel, a visionary who recognized, profoundly, that our wounds and those of the world are ultimately one. What that suggests is that our larger allegiances must be to one another, past the narrow-heartedness of loyalty to any particular nation-state. After all, as the big-thinking and generously spirited Einstein put it, bluntly, nationalism is finally "an infantile disease ...the measles of humankind."

Ultimately, daring to care about the pain of others is not an option, but a shrewd form of self-preservation. For as Martin Luther King, Jr., reminds us, "injustice anywhere is a threat to justice everywhere." How it is, then, that we are told never to forget 9/11 and the nearly 3,000 innocent lives taken, and yet in the same breath we never remember the unjust "war" exacted in retribution and the hundreds of thousands of Iraqi civilian lives killed in the process? If we can agree that all human life is sacred, we must insist that all murder is unholy. Like American soldier-poet Brian Turner tells us in his devastating report from Iraq, *Here, Bullet*: "it should break your heart to kill... nightmare you."

If we choose to turn our back to the wailing of our suffering world, and carry on amusing ourselves to death, violence like a karmic serpent will wind its way to our doorstep. If we wonder, cynically, *Why should we care about Palestine the way we do about Ukraine?* how can we avoid finding ourselves confronted with protests in our schools? Or police brutality in our communities, gun violence and the unhealed horrors of race relations in America? Or the unstoppable plaintive cry as old as the creation of a nation of American Indians at Standing Rock? Or physically and psychologically damaged war vets who, we tell ourselves "fought for our freedom"? Or the problems of homelessness and uprootedness? Or the growing numbers of refugees seeking—like our ancestors, wherever they came from—peace and freedom? Or terrorists of all sorts who have taken the shape of our shadows? What are these but the unsettling side-effects of our pandemic of indifference?

If all this does not wake the sleepwalker, they are confronted with another type of disruption: the eruption of hateful reactionary politics at the voting booths in the US and across Europe, driven by leaders without vision or integrity who don't reflect our nobler longings and disregard the better angels of our nature. If we don't speak in unison and declare: *Not in our name*, we will find ourselves cutting off our nose to spite our face, shooting ourselves in one foot and chewing on the other... while waiting for the world to change. But here's the truth: we can't bury pain and not expect it to grow roots. What we can do is try to attend, tenderly, to its bitter-sweet fruits.

"The creative adult is the child who has survived," as Ursula K. Le Guin reminds us. Over time, I've come to be fascinated by moral or spiritual wounds and how best to put them to use. What if we were to view our wounds as peepholes through which to view the world's wounds and tend to the wounds of others – and our planet – as an extension of our larger body? These words from Leonard Cohen's "Anthem" became my own when he called us to "Ring the bells that still can ring / Forget your perfect offering / There is a crack in everything / That's how the light gets in."

Long before him, another virtuoso of suffering, Sufi mystic Rumi, voiced this timeless insight: "The wound is the place where the light enters you." If the wound is where the light enters us, then how can we keep our wounds clean? One way is to recognize that we are all wounded—and wounding. And to remember that exceptionalism is dangerous nonsense that enables us to inflict pain on others, knowingly and unknowingly. If this is so, we might try to forgive damaged people (including ourselves) since they can hardly imagine the pain they inflict on others.

Another human perversion comes to mind when we see how bullies seek to play the role of victims. I look at the dangerous folly of the Middle

East, and I look at the self-defeating arrogance and self-congratulatory ignorance of the United States, and what I see is this: the same gaping world-wound, bleeding because it is not being compassionately dressed. We need a different approach, one rooted in a deeper wisdom, to connect with one another at the place of our wounds and try to heal, together. As American psychiatrist Morgan Scott Peck put it:

> *How strange that we should ordinarily feel compelled to hide our wounds when we are all wounded! Community requires the ability to expose our wounds and weaknesses to our fellow creatures. It also requires the ability to be affected by the wounds of others... But even more important is the love that arises among us when we share, both ways, our woundedness.*

We forgive to live. Because, as an Arab-American bridge of a man by the name of Gibran reminds us: "Hate is a dead thing. Who of you would be a tomb?"

This collection attempts to answer to that haunting question. The poems you are about to read move across the difficult, pained arc from bursts of anguish, anger, and despair towards a more resilient hope. From noisy political entanglement towards a quieter spiritual surrender–in recognition of the inescapable truth that we are One and suffer when we forget this. The future we all long for is far more than mere cessation of violence (though surely this is a needed first step). Rather, our shared goal has to do with becoming those who commit themselves, "in the midst of darkness / and ugliness" to be among the ones who "hungered / for light and beauty."

In the poems that follow, I wonder how it is we readily accept that we are governed by physical laws like gravity yet believe that we can turn our backs on age-old spiritual laws like Love, Compassion, Forgiveness, Mercy, Trust, Hope without paying a high and deadly price. What if we were to consider that each time we betray our conscience, we strangle an angel? Keeping in mind that it is not at all certain that we are allotted an infinite supply of winged pardons.

When the encroaching darkness proved too great and words failed to offer solace, during the ethnic cleansing and genocide of Palestinians, I turned to art. Specially, I turned to the visual arts for consolation, such as the elegiac elegance of Palestinian painter and national treasure, Sliman Mansour. More than a few times, in the waking nightmare of these nearly unbearable times, I've found sustenance in the iconic cover art by Mansour: depicting a Palestinian mother surrounded by her small children in the tranquil setting of their village. The woman is gazing up with longing at the star-festooned night sky, which some children seem to be reaching out for. This dreamy painting is three-fourths glowing sky, one-fourth muted land, and hovering above the maternal figure, luminous like a moon, is a giant dove carrying an olive branch. Mansour's serene painting is fittingly titled "Symbol of Hope," a reminder that, even amid death, destruction and deprivation, there is Indestructible Beauty. Hope, after all, is more natural, resilient, and patient than despair, and so outlasts it.

Hope

Hope's not quite as it seems,
it's slimmer than you'd think
and less steady on its feet.

Sometimes, it's out of breath
can hardly see ahead
and cries itself to sleep.

It may not tell you all this
or the times it cheated death
but, if you knew it, you'd know

how Hope can keep a secret.

I
Unbearable Casualties

PALESTINE WAIL

What to Bring to a War Protest

Bring a candle
burning in your eyes
to lead the way,

bring a bird
nestled in your heart
to set others free

bring a shroud
large enough to bury
the dead past

bring a flag
spotless and white
to surrender pain.

Alternative Scenario

After the horrors of October 7
the good people of Palestine rushed
to the side of stricken Israelis

Tending to the wounded,
mourning the dead,
comforting survivors

They kept vigil, praying & weeping
delivering truckloads of flowers
serving trays, by day, of warm meals & sweets

Palestinian families flooded the streets
en masse, protesting: *Not in our Names*
demanding the return of hostages

Recognizing the great need, they gifted
what they, too, longed for: mercy, solace, solidarity–
and the world, witnessing, never forgot...

Helpless, Hamas eventually surrendered,
the Israeli government, in turn, relented
and walls in hearts crumbled, then tumbled.

Open Letter to Israel

> *He who fights monsters should see to it that, in the process,*
> *he does not become a monster.*
> — Nietzsche

Tell me, what steel entered your heart,
what fear made you rabid,
what hate drove out pity?

How could you forget
that how we fight a battle
determines who we become?
When did you grow reckless
with the state of your soul?

We are responsible for our enemy,
compassion is to consider the role
that we play in their creation.

If you prick us, do we not bleed?
...If you poison us, do we not die?
And if you wrong us, shall we not revenge?

Strange, how one hate enables another;
how they are like unconscious allies,
darkly united in blocking out the Light.

Yes, we can lend ideas our breath, but ideals —
Peace, Justice, Freedom — require our entire lives
and, all who are tormented by such ideals
must learn to make an ally of humility.

Truth, and conscience, can be like large, bothersome flies
— brush them away and they return, buzzing louder
tens of thousands slaughtered, half of whom are children
no, these are unbearable casualties to ignore

To speak nothing of the intangible casualties:
damage done to our collective psyche, trust, and sleep
no more nightmares, please, give us back our dreams
we can still begin, again, and must
wisdom is a return to innocence.

The Exodus Continues...

"Where will we go?"
pleaded the Palestinian
displaced six times since Oct. 7.

Every time we return to our homes
and begin to rebuild our lives,
even on the rubble of our houses,
the occupation sends back
tanks to destroy what is left

This is the hideous reality
9 months of war delivered —
where Palestinians not eradicated
are herded like bewildered cattle

Condemned as wandering Jews
to roam the world and meditate
upon their unforgiveable sin
and the vengeance of victims.

PALESTINE WAIL

Family Fatality

A towering ship looms
in the heavy night –
slow-moving towards
a restless shore

Navigating inky dark,
it steers clear of milky light
thrown by a full moon…
steadily, it advances, stealthily

Has it come to collect
a long-standing debt
finally, to take me Home
helpless, against my will?

Air & Sea Show

The air is a storm of pitiless steel birds
the terrible beauty of fighter planes
mimicking natural flight formations
with unholy, and thunderous cries

Pirouetting and swooping awfully low
ruffling the feathers of real birds
and small children on the beach below
as they cower in stupefied awe

At times of an alleged war, on intelligence
there's no swallowing the bitter taste
of smoke, left by these flying guns –
these decorative killing machines

As they elegantly perforate an azure sky
with surgical precision and crude power
a frankly obscene display of military might
or the arrogance of shock and aw, shucks

What corruption of the freedom of flying
and the democratic innocence of amusement fairs
these screeching pterosaurs, branded "blue angels"
O, how they blaspheme . . .

Why Care?

Because you did not have to run out to hunt
for a spare tent in the middle of the night
    – chest-constricted and frantic –
lucky, you and your family
were not obliterated
by the raining bombs

demolishing your home
snatching your childhood memories
replacing them with an unholy stench

of burning human flesh.

Columbia University

Student encampments mushroom
across American college campuses
registering overdue protests
against corrupt governments
here and there and us
for failing them...

Sites of the uneasy conscience
of the divided states of America
where students are the teachers

Bless these natural born idealists
(in other words, peace activists)
for their unbridled vision
and unbribable principles

Bless the young for reminding us
there is no looking away
no foreign soil
no Others.

How to Protest

It is, infinitely, tricky
to embody an Ideal:

Truth, Beauty, Justice, Peace
are not at all easy to wear

Anger, even righteous, can
wear us out and soon devolve
into its opposite: violent hate

What is life-sustaining,
like milk, will curdle if left
unattended, in the heat.

Stranger in a Strange Land

America is a psychopath,
a gaslighting, abusive partner
that insists on being loved
no, worshipped as saint and savior

Never mind your murdered family
lying at your feet and bloody knife
still clutched in their hands…

It wasn't always this way,
look, what you made me do!
Don't make me do it, again –
smile and try to be grateful.

Wounded Healers

Lately, when I see
a beautiful person,
I want to ask them:
who or what hurt you?

Because I recognize
they had to work hard
in dark caves to carve
space for such a Light.

Yet what is freedom
or transformation
but a lifelong practice
of the art of dying?

At Gaza Zoo

humans & animals
shelter side by side
starving & shell-shocked

lions, parrots, monkeys
men, women, children
all fearing for their lives
all uncertain about tomorrow

Living among animals
is more merciful
than warplanes in the sky.

The zookeepers are nearly dead.

PALESTINE WAIL

During a Genocide

You will find that during a genocide
most words lose their meaning –
some sound empty & others strange

Apart from unceasing prayer,
eloquence takes the form
of tears or kindness and solidarity

Even a quiet moan or sighing
is preferable to false words or worse:
a loud and wounding Silence...

Palestinian Music

For more than a hundred days,
in a daze, I read & wrote of Gaza
stunned, overwhelmed, indignant

Yet, all along, unable to cry
(I don't know why)
until, today…

Listening to Palestinian music
I wept, helplessly, at the pity,
longing, waste of it all & weep still.

Ceasefire

What a blood-thirsty world...
when calling for ceasefire
is considered controversial

Yet, our divided world remains
indivisible & when we murder,
we destroy a part of our souls.

Waking Nightmares

How is it that
life carries on,
as they cry for us,
from under the rubble?

While doctors amputate
limbs without anesthesia,
how did we staunch the wounds
of our own throbbing hearts?

The watermelons are rotten
– cut open and bone dry –
from bleeding in the streets

Watered tears, I shudder to imagine
the future of these sad seeds,
what terrible fruit will grow…

Starving

When did we learn
starvation is acceptable
as a form of punishment?

Go to your room,
children are told
no dinner for you

Today, we witness
Palestinians denied food,
dignity or even mercy

When can they leave
their prison cells,
occupied since birth?

Palestinian Diet

Devastating that starving Palestinians
are now forced to eat animal feed,
but not without significance:

Donkeys as beasts of burden
represent stubborn endurance,
rabbits fertility and rebirth,
pigeons freedom and peace

Does this dehumanizing diet
hold keys to their transformation?

The Limits of Love

You're welcome to a small helping
of care, a portion of our concern
Ache, if you like, but don't cry
on our shoulder, for overlong

Please, help yourself and move on
or you may find yourself, abruptly
at the outskirts of compassion
by the fence, where barbed wire begins

There is a sign that you can't miss:
Keep out, it reads, in blood red;
Private territory, trespassers
will be shot with indifference.

Resume

No matter how exalted your mission statement

Servant of an Inscrutable God,
Restorer of historical injustice
Protector of a Chosen People,
Champion of Existence's underdogs

there are two small words that will spoil
the most aspirational resume
and forever tarnish your reputation

Those damning words are: child-killer.

Overwhelming Emotion

Why do we open our mouth
when in shock or struck
by unbearable grief?

Why do we cover our lips
with our hand, in pity
or in great sorrow?

What are we preventing
from getting in or out —
other than useless words?

You Win by Losing

Awoke, in the middle of the night
with these words ringing in my ears:

You win (morally, spiritually)
by losing (on the physical plane)

O, Gaza, O, Palestine ...
you had to be exterminated

to be seen & remembered.

The Elephant in the Room

How polite our friends
the way that they avoid
mention of complicated affairs
      – Palestinian and Israeli –

Is it because they find it rude
to talk Murder over dinner
or do they see this bloody mess
as terribly embarrassing

A drawn-out family feud...
which, in a sense, it is.

Q&A

The answer to the question
is invariably one
of the following:

patience,
forgiveness,
sacrifice,
hope,
gratitude,
prayer…
in other words, love.

If each of us houses the Divine,
then to take another's life
is to murder a piece of G_d.

PALESTINE WAIL

Who is Innocent?

If one were hard of heart
they might ask
is any Israeli innocent

In a state where military
is compulsory for all
are there any citizens

Is Israel really a democracy
or just another theocracy
blinded by a too literal faith

How can any freedom be
built upon another's captivity
the jailor is never free

But by the same harsh logic
one must condemn every Palestinian
for the stone in their hand or heart

Who is innocent since Cain
took his brother Abel's life—
whoever is able can live better

In Hebrew, Cain means possessor,
while Abel means empty...
what does that mean, today

If we have no peace
Mother Teresa reminds us
it's because we have forgotten

We belong to each other.

Gaza, Capital of Hurt

Fitting that the word gauze
should have ties to Gaza (غزة)

a center of weaving
since the 13th century

It's our turn, after hundreds of years
to dress Gazan wounds & wipe their tears...

What Tragedy Teaches Us

Our friends fall into different camps:
those who feel our pain as their own
— without hesitation or calculation —
will rush to our side,
casting their lot with ours
seeking to heal

Others, tested by fire
or tempted by the world,
we must try to forgive:
whose tongues are tied
or hands are bound,
by an unspeakable doubt
or allegiance to another pain

At least, they wish us no harm
& if they do, they do not know
us or themselves well enough...
forgiveness only matters,
Derrida argued,
if we forgive the unforgivable

If you and I cannot remain friends,
because we do not see eye to eye,
how can we call for peace in our world?

Pity the Looters

Those who feel unseen and unheard
whose hopes and dignity have been robbed

They do not take pride in their nation
because its laws and leaders fill them with shame

What's the value of broken glass or twisted steel
compared to a soul that's been crushed?

They are presumed guilty until proven guilty
their only birthright is humiliation

Those with nothing left to lose
desperate, take what they can.

The old world is dying, said Gramsci;
the new world struggles to be born:

now is the time of monsters.

PALESTINE WAIL

Blasphemous Praise

The poet is a prophet:
a fisher of souls,
a human sacrifice,
sent to save you

an undoer of knots,
your sworn advocate,
a life-long listener,
a reminder when you forget

your unknown friend,
a helper in affliction,
and with your consent,
a trusted healer.

Choices

It's difficult, in times like these
not to become radicalized –
the question is: will it be
by all consuming hate or Pity?

Fever Dream

Every bed a raft
tossed at sea
afraid of what
lurks beneath

We do not float
but are connected
to the sea floor
like islands

Self-sufficient,
inter-dependent—
only paradoxes
can be trusted.

No sleep, now
only dreaming...
in the deep end,
every stroke counts

Time to read,
then write and
rewrite our will
(as in willpower).

The Eclipse

Where were you
during the apocalypse
on the other side
of the world?

Did you pause
to observe
a moment of silence?

Did the extermination
of the other half
interrupt your sleep?

Did their absence,
somehow, disturb
your festivities?

Did you notice
the eclipse
is here to stay?

Radical Love

Radical love understands
#freethehostages means
all Palestinians living
under an inhumane occupation

2 million innocent souls in Gaza
1/2 of whom are bewildered
children under the age of 18
being collectively punished

– denied water, electricity,
medicines & mercy –
in one of the most densely populated
spaces on earth, casually,
known as an 'open air prison'

#standwithisrael means denouncing
700,000 Israeli settlers,
since who understands better
the curse of homelessness
and wandering in the wilderness

#supportIsrael means disowning
apartheid, ethic cleansing, genocide
because we solemnly swore, before
as one human family: *Nevermore*

#bringthemhome refers to the right
of return for some 14 million Palestinians,
scattered throughout an indifferent world

Radical love understands
there is no October 7, 2023
without May 15, 1948,
our September 11th...

Summary

The hands were made to clasp
the knees designed to bend
the body created to pray.

What else is there to say?

The mouth was shaped to gasp
the eyes drawn to attend
the soul commanded to obey.

What else is there to say?

The memory was wired to lapse
the heart fashioned to rend
the will inclined to betray

What else is there to say?

Say Something

If you're uncomfortable saying Genocide,

say mass murder,
say boneyard,
say unmarked graves,
say pity the children
say humanity under the rubble...
say Lord, forgive us
the enormity of our sins

At least, say not in my name
I'm waiting to hear from you

Please, say something.

II

Lingering at the Threshold

PALESTINE WAIL

You, Again

You again, of the singing wound
here again, lost and found and lost
trafficking in metaphysics and eternity
as the nearest hopes

where to, pilgrim
outdistancing chasms
rationing emotions
seeking sustenance

for the self too subtle and proud
for words
nocturnal flower, nurtured solitude
watered night

there you go, restraining the impulse
to say it all at once
even surrounded by silence
still filled with noise

now, having stirred some thrumming
hour when the moon throws
her full-bodied light
over all, like a silver screen night
of silent films, the whirring
of the reel.

11th Hour Plea

One foot here, one foot there
how much longer, weary pilgrim,
lingering at the threshold?

One step forward, two steps back
-still lusting after this world-
Have you forgotten your promises?

To die to your self, to transmute
the mud to gold, to surrender
distractions and consent to be born?

Practice

The daily struggle
to seek clarity
in this smoke-filled world

Instead of poetry as piety
poets compete for intimacy
with some abyss...

Clean, Bright

The light you emanate,
intermittently,
—that attracts many,
and guides a few—
does not belong to you.

Please, don't diminish it
with selfish desires
so what was meant
to illuminate heavens,
sputters in the gutters.

PALESTINE WAIL

For Israel, Palestine & the Human Family

To regain our innocence, we must surrender
our cherished degree in demonology
renounce all intimate familiarity
with those wily spirits of destruction.

In our defense against the howling
seductive entreaties of the night
we might clutch childhood's mascots, and all our love
fiercely against our trembling chest.

Peace, Lily

In the midst of a genocide,
our Peace Lily began to bloom

For years, it withheld its flowers,
but sensing a great need

it could not bear it any longer
& granted us radiant relief.

Hunter and Hunted

The Work, whether employed or not
has been trying to remain
creatively, spiritually alive

Herding words, gathering world
spinning a wheel-shaped web
out of oneself and waiting

To catch something of sustenance
wrap it in silk and ingest it
so one might dream, again.

Ramadan

It is not merely food
one renounces while fasting,
but thoughtlessness.

To fast is to slow down
almost to a stillness
and distill what is necessary:

sacrifice, patience, obedience
– in other words, radical gratitude.

PALESTINE WAIL

By Definition

A martyr is a witness
who testifies and gives evidence
only in a Higher Court

They must suffer death
because otherworldly truth
requires sacrifice of this life.

Lamentations

Write me a book
of lamentations
passionate and profound
pure expressions

of loss and longing
and you will discover
true sorrow is sacred
and your songs are psalms.

Ode to the Children

It is wrong to believe
the children of Palestine
are, somehow, cursed —
they are blessed

as are their torn families
and fallen homes
schools and places of worship

there is an ancient connection
between sacredness
and sacrificial acts

originally, to "bless" meant
to consecrate or make holy
by marking with blood

as seen in religious rituals
like Passover or Eid al-Adha
(also known as Feast of Sacrifice)
where doorposts were blessed
with lamb's blood

the blood of Palestine's children
symbolizes sanctification
and protection from evil
and God knows best.

Imagine That

animals have eternal souls
giving praise in tongues
unknown to us
belonging to communities
that also receive
divinely sent messages.

PALESTINE WAIL

What to Say, First

say silence
say longing
say awe
say spirit
say light

say pity
say humanity
say humility
say helpless
say ignorance
say patience

say repentance
say sacrifice
say forgiveness
say mercy
say obedience
say grace
say peace

say atone
say work
say charity
say hope
say praise
say belief
say faith
say devotion

say love
say surrender
say rebirth
say trust
say holy
say miracle
say amen
before you can
say religion
or utter the word:

G_d.

Confessions

A mystic is a tormented soul who surrenders
the turmoil of violent passions to the Lord
– entrusts Him alone with their burning body

The spiritual journey is one of great risk
in perpetual danger of spilling over...
a long night of wild terror precedes safety

Proceed with caution, pilgrim,
you have been, gravely warned:
Here, moral harm is immortal.

Minister of Loneliness

I wonder what are the qualifications
for such a lamentable post,
what lessons learned can be shared;
how might such a job description read?

Prospective applicants must be intimate
with isolation, desolation, desperation
able to minister to moral injury
or spiritual woundedness

Please, attach a portfolio of personal relations
that have not ended badly,
and, if they have, how have you
bounced back, sidestepping abysses

Tell us, do you recognize loneliness
as a public health crisis
Can you decipher the subtle clues
of this insidious pandemic?

Successful candidates must be virtuosos of suffering
sensitive, of course, yet impervious to lingering sadness
tirelessly capable of encouraging others despite,
at times, feeling defeated or assaulted by pointlessness

If appointed, what would you do differently
from the previous three Ministers of Loneliness
who struggled with this title? How will you overcome
that loneliness of perpetual sociability?

Are you willing and able to work alongside
those unacknowledged ministers of loneliness
mystics, poets and artists of all stripes
who serve this role, quietly, without credit?

Lastly, candidates must agree to submit
to a lie detector test, to prove that
their online friendships are satisfying,
and posts of smiling selfies or social media persona
are not, in fact, an elaborate fabrication.

Spirit Diary

There is a place in us all
that is beyond self and pain

a space of wonder and gratitude
where we must strive to arrive
and, once there, to meet others

But, first we must pass through fire
and all its seductive monsters.

A House Divided

I was in a life-long rush
because I could not guess
when I might self-combust

From sunrise to sunset
I tried to run fast and far
to outdistance disaster

But I was never free
to be other than me
or reset a date with fate

I was never given
one secure day to live in
without self-sabotage

So part of me carefully built
a makeshift shelter from the storm
while another part dismantled it

Meantime, I learned to pray
and repeat, by night and by day:
Heaven save us from ourselves.

Re: Birth

So, what does it mean to be reborn?
It's having to relearn the basics:
how to walk, talk and eat...our words

Did we ever imagine the day when
we would have to be taught, as adults,
how to wash our hands...of our sins?

Time to sit, in humility, listen
and assume that we, really, know nothing.

So, what does it feel like
to be grounded, globally

sent to our rooms
like errant children

privileges suspended
and told to think hard

about why we got here
and how we'll get out?

Tell me, what's your exit plan?

PALESTINE WAIL

Purity

Renounce all violence
of heart, word and deed—
only the blameless shall lead

Visionaries of this age,
like prophets of ages past,
are the moral reformers.

Prayer Without Hands

As a younger person, mastering your craft
– balancing bicycle against self –
you might, miraculously, lift your hands
from the handlebars and propel yourself
using only your weight and will.

It's the same with prayer in older age...
on cold nights when you are swaddled,
like a helpless child in bed,
your arms pinned to your side
and prayer beads out of reach.

You might worship, motionlessly–
addressing the Unknowable One
(whatever you can imagine, He is not)
and find yourself, mysteriously uplifted
without ever raising a finger.

PALESTINE WAIL

Fine, Tuning

Whatever else artists might be
– monster, angel, prophet,
battleground or burial ground–
they are also tuning forks;
struck at every turn and
sounding out the worlds.

I Get It, Now

Reviewing the drama of my life,
sometimes I pause and wonder
was this or that incident intended
for my enjoyment or torment?

How about this or that person
do they represent pleasure or pain?
And I smile, bitter-sweetly
knowing, at heart, that one cannot

see anything in isolation...
Angels wrestle with demons
in an eternal dance
for our betterment.

PALESTINE WAIL

Sigh

Mother tongue of the soul
a sigh needs no translation
universal breath

Past words
over their heads
quietly heard
noble air

Swirls of ether
yarns of yearning

Melancholy music
played by the spirit
on the harp strings
of the heart

Sighs escape
unguarded

Proofs of endurance
evidence of excess luggage
plaintive protests
wrapped in acceptance
wistful winds on wings

From the depths
to the heights

They hover in the air
rise and return
in the form of rain
when clouds sigh, in turn
and wash us clean, again
with their tears.

Eros & Thanatos

We live, love and create
as best as we can
but, sometimes, in haste
— lest we succumb
to the siren call
of self-destruction.

Learning to Pray

Long susceptible to the pious heresies,
of mystics, martyrs and other fanatics
mad enough to confound themselves
with G_d, and declare it free of ego

Those spiritually reckless creatures
contemptuous of all rule books,
traffic signs and speeding tickets
in such a hurry were they to arrive

No social drinkers, these revelers
they drank to get drunk, alone
that they might stay that way
—sobriety being the only sin

But what of us without stamina
for such superhuman attention
or the patience to stand in line
inching towards the checkout

Might we forge our own language
(until we can speak in tongues)
by asking of our every action:
does this, or that, please You?

Lectio Divina

Unconsciously, I have practiced
for years—a lifetime, really—
reading as a mysterious way
to meditate and almost pray

Slowing down to a stillness
to discern the Divine voice
I have written verse
(or something like it)
in a blessed trance...

These signposts for living well
I have shared, freely, with the world
and, more deliberately, with myself.

Double Bind

To secure the world's sympathy
Palestinians must be saintly –
yet, Israel has universal trust
despite continuing to act monstrously.

Now, tell us the difference
between Palestinians & Hamas?
I sigh and say, again, Palestinians
are an innocent people
who want only to live in peace

Caught between a rock, called Israel,
and a hard place that is Hamas.

Two Types of Kisses

What is a mystic
but one who swoons,
defenseless
in the face of beauty

A natural believer
in evolution of spirit.

Two types of kisses,
and the choice is yours:
either with burning lips,
that bind and blind

Or a lipless kind,
preparing us to leave
a too-tight skin behind.

I stand, helpless, before
the sensuality of stretches,
but get down on bended knee
for the spiritual variety.

PALESTINE WAIL

III

On a Far Shore

PALESTINE WAIL

Poems Sailing

I sent my poem sailing in the sky
and it did not make me rich,
but it landed on a far shore
and taught children to make a wish

I sent more of my poems out to sea
and they did not bring me a wife –
yet guided fishermen home in a storm
and by helping others, they saved my life.

Inventory

When it comes to worldly
& spiritual successes,
I am the king of near misses:

connoisseur of almost glory,
intimate with virtual ruin

For my ongoing humiliations,
I assume sole blame –

yet for these underserved blessings,
credit a greater Name.

PALESTINE WAIL

Love That Makes Devils Weep

Meditating on a nearly impossible
possibility: what would it take to end
a war, to absolve ancient animosities

What would it look like, if one side
resolved to be entirely blameless.
even when provoked, relentlessly

Until the other side relented helplessly,
realizing there was nothing left to fear
but the corruption of their own soul

How could such purity of heart be denied,
once one party surrendered entirely
might that not make devils weep?

Middle East Advice

To begin a conversation
about Palestine & Israel
first, you must say:

I am your brother
& you are my sister

I am sorry
how we wronged
ourselves
& the human family

Then, you can speak of history
and compare your losses

Finally, you must embrace
in pity
and be silent.

Garden Meditation

For hours in the morning sun
I knelt over our plants,
like a prayer carpet

Devoted to weeding our garden
I sweat, squint and grunt
marveling at the tenacity of living things

How stubborn neglected weeds can be
clinging for dear life, like bad habits...
over time, almost stitched to the earth

Yes, some were undeniably alluring
not unlike our sly, deceitful sins—
evil masquerading as good

Prompting us to dig deeper
seeking the root – to eliminate
what is undesirable from returning

Remarkable interconnectedness
unfathomable, delicate balance
not least, the role of the lowly worm

How it quietly, steadily turns the soil
assisting water and nutrients to flow
like our own out-of-sight soul work

After the rain, the dirt yields
to such spiritual pruning –
the way tears soften hardened hearts.

Exhaling

I read less, lately,
and most days, don't write
or try to, but sit
and let the air out

so I might slowly fall
to the ocean floor
and let the depths
have their way with me.

Consider This

The muezzin
calling you to prayer
might be a musician
or a poet

the minaret
of a mosque
could be a page
or a stage.

Reaching

Yes, my Other, this is how
I always recognize you
Upward-reaching, and glad
within wing's wind of a Great Song.

The Lightkeepers

Hope is a lighthouse
(or, at least, a lamppost)
someone must keep vigil
to illumine this possibility

In the dark, a poet will climb
narrow, unsteady stairs
to gaze past crashing waves
and sing to us new horizons

Others, less far-sighted, might
be deceived by the encroaching night
mistake the black for lasting, but
not those entrusted with trimming wicks

Their tasks are more pressing –
winding clockworks, replenishing oil –
there is no time for despair
when tending to the Light.

Prayer Beads

The mystery of the worlds
held in your hands
oscillating between Here
and the Hereafter

With rhythmic movement,
an undulating thumb
and steadfast forefinger,
prostrate and stand at attention

Losing self and time, in trance,
navigating immeasurable spaces
at once, grounded and at sea —
nameless as the summoned One

Worlds at your fingertips
each bead an orbiting planet
or a patient Muslim pilgrim
circumambulating Mecca's Kaaba.

In Praise of Fruit

Fruits are like poems
they drop to the ground
or blush on branches
to tell us they're ready

Gratitude does not waste blessings
nature will first offer these
to more attentive others,
before collecting them herself

Better to salvage such gifts
when they are fragrant, ripe
make a bouquet of fruits – poems
to nourish body and spirit.

Tell me,

who's to say where poetry
starts and where it ends?

said another scribbler-in-the-margins
of that great book of Longing.

Secrets

Can we ever write about secrets
that we cannot speak of
the thing or two that determine
who we are and what we do

when can we hint at the harm
we've hardly survived
the realization that our allure
is due to deformity?

Sure, we confess in code
here, there and everywhere
beneath our breaths
and over their heads

But when can we ever speak,
plainly, of our obscene pain
to whom and how might we
unburden ourselves, artlessly?

The answer might be never
whispers art, to which we owe all
—our lives, wisdom and masks —
only transformation will set us free.

I Ran

I ran hard and far
to outdistance my pain
But, when I got lost
my pain found me –
caressed me, wordlessly
and carried me Home.

Destinations

There are books, like experiences,
that measure our distances
and cannot be read until
we reach their remote shores.

Walls

Walls cannot contain
the human spirit –
they cannot hold back love
or keep out hate…

Humanity exists on either end
and it's a violence
against the human family
to pick a side

Those who build walls
and condone them
do not understand
the limitless heart.

Relent

The spiritual answer is:

Don't blame anyone,
for anything –

Not others, life,
least of all, God.

Accept the blame,
let it be your teacher.

For John

I believe a leaf of grass is no less than the journey-work of the stars.
—Walt Whitman

❦ There are leaves & petals strewn
on my bedroom & bathroom floor,
as if I'd returned from sleepwalking
in the woods which, in a sense, I had.

The stroll, with my almost 3-year-old nephew,
ended up being more of an extended bow—
as the awestruck child knelt, reverently,
to gather bits of nature into my pocket.

The green called out to him, wildly & he
responded, exuberantly, collecting
what he could fit into his small palms:

a pretty orange flower, for Lisa,
his sister, who stayed behind
and tiny berries, he called apples

Everything was new, important
and worthy of closer inspection...
a poem is what makes you smile,
when you are alone. ❦

Hush

Intervals granted between revelation
are for prophets to catch their breath

To integrate the Divine Word
– glad tidings and warnings –
into this world takes time and effort

Holy Silence is a test
of endurance and mercy.

Hungering

In the midst of darkness
and ugliness,
I hungered
for light and beauty

I found it
reading and writing –
poetry, mysticism,
then silence.

Afterword: Poetry of Resistance and Resilience

> I wish children didn't die.
> I wish they would be temporarily elevated
> to the skies until the war ends.
>
> Then they would return home safe,
> And when their parents would ask them,
> where were you? They would say,
> we were playing in the clouds.
>
> – Palestinian artist & activist Ghassan Kanafani
> (1936–1972)

The death of one child, due to natural causes, is nearly unbearable. The systematic, cold-blooded murder of thousands of innocent children, in the name of so-called "self-defense," is an unjustifiable moral obscenity. Yet this is what the Israeli government continues to do, and it is appalling that there remain democratic nations as well as civilized individuals who find it difficult to unequivocally condemn such depravity and call for a ceasefire. Who will honor these blameless, anonymous martyrs? How can we remain silent in the face of such atrocities, when even the good Lord has this to say about the sins of indifference in the book of Revelations:

> So then, because you are lukewarm, and neither cold nor hot,
> I will vomit you out of my mouth. [Revelation 3:16]

Thank God, the true artist is neither deceived nor cowed by herd mentality. An artist of this exalted station serves simultaneously as an unblinking witness, a voice for the voiceless, an archivist of longing and memory, in short, as a prophet who gives voice to our collective conscience. Words matter, since narratives shape realities – and, in turn, how history is told and who is deemed worthy of our sympathies. That's why artists are considered dangerous – for daring to speak truth to power. It is especially significant, then, that since October 7, 2023, around 100 Palestinian journalists have been killed in Gaza alone, all serving in the line of duty, while Israel has murdered nearly 30 Palestinian artists, intellectuals, and writers in Gaza.

Our understanding of the human condition is diminished without the emotionally imaginative and spiritually enriching witness of storytellers and artists. We know from watching the news that narratives are grossly distorted when hijacked by corrupt politicians and compromised media. As a prominent figure in the Civil Rights movement in the United States, Malcolm X succinctly put it this way: "If you're not careful, the newspapers will have you hating the people who are being oppressed, and loving the people who are doing the oppressing." A case in point is the murder of young Palestinian poet, scholar and activist, Dr. Refaat Alareer, who was assassinated by a targeted Israeli airstrike, along with his brother, sister and her four children.

Anticipating his death, Alareer reshared on social media his heart-rending poem, just one month prior to being killed by Israeli forces:

If I must die

If I must die,
you must live
to tell my story
to sell my things
to buy a piece of cloth
and some strings,
(make it white with a long tail)
so that a child, somewhere in Gaza
while looking heaven in the eye
awaiting his dad who left in a blaze –
and bid no one farewell
not even to his flesh
not even to himself –
sees the kite, my kite you made, flying up above
and thinks for a moment an angel is there
bringing back love
If I must die
let it bring hope
let it be a tale

For the names of these martyrs to remain a blessing, and for their deaths not to be in vain, they must live on among us by being transformed into tales that give us hope and courage to ward off that great deceiver: despair.

Another Palestinian poet, activist, and martyr, Ghassan Kanafani, innately understood that for the Palestinian cause to resonate worldwide, it was important to frame the struggle against imperialism as a global one: "[it] laid its body over the world, the head in Eastern Asia, the heart in the Middle East, its arteries reaching Africa and Latin America. Wherever you strike it, you damage it, and you serve the World Revolution." Because truth agrees with itself across time and space, here is an echo by yet another assassinated activist and celebrated civil rights leader, Martin Luther King, Jr., who spoke eloquently on behalf of the interconnectedness of all human struggles: "We are caught in an inescapable network of mutuality, tied in a single garment of destiny. Whatever affects one directly, affects all indirectly." Mercifully, the number of people of conscience denouncing the criminal acts of the current Israeli government, as well as the blind and disgraceful support of the United States of America, is increasing, despite the great personal risk involved in speaking out.

Josh Paul, a former Director at the US State Department's Bureau of Political Military Affairs, resigned on principle (October 18, 2023) after serving eleven years in an office responsible for the transfer of arms to allies. In his resignation letter, Paul addressed his moral quandary regarding the United States' excessive and unquestioning military support to Israel, also hinting at widespread internal discomfort regarding the US administration's complicity in the indiscriminate murder of Palestinians. Paul summed up the hypocrisy of US foreign policy, reminding us that "[w]e cannot be both against occupation, and for it. We cannot be both for freedom, and against it. And we cannot be for a better world, while contributing to one that is materially worse."

Amid the rampant fear, hatred and misinformation fueling the current war-mongering there are two important Jewish voices speaking out on behalf of compassion and justice. Norman Finkelstein and Gabor Maté are both children of Holocaust survivors and yet they have dared to care for the plight of Palestinians and condemn the state-sanctioned cruelty Israel continues to inflict upon a people "more sinned against than sinning."

Finkelstein is unafraid to call a spade a spade, characterizing the situation in Palestine as a genocide, while Maté is clear that there can be no peace moving forward without an end to Israel's vicious assault on Gaza and its preparation for an illegal occupation. In a remarkable interview with comedian Russell Brand, Maté was unambiguous regarding his solidarity with the Palestinian people: "You don't have to support Hamas policies to stand up for Palestinian rights....Take the worst thing you can say about Hamas multiplied by a thousand times, and you still will not meet the Israeli repression, and killing, and dispossession of Palestinians."

Both Finkelstein and Maté are erudite intellectuals and passionate activists in the tradition of Kanafani, who bring a wealth of experience to their understanding of the Palestinian Cause. Finkelstein has devoted forty years of his life to a close study of the Middle East, while Maté is a renowned intergenerational-trauma therapist. For those who continue to pretend that the world began on October 7 – such as journalist Piers Morgan – these learned and compassionate voices can put the Palestinian trauma into historical context, reminding us that there can be no lasting peace founded on injustice and that the jailor is never free.

But it should not require any special education to be outraged by the daily horrors taking place in the Gaza Strip, a land that is a fraction of the size of the smallest US state, Rhode Island, and one of the most densely populated regions in the world, often now referred to as 'the world's largest open-air prison.' It is enough simply to be a concerned member of the human family, to ask ourselves *how might we feel if we were in their place*, in order to share Kanafani's outrage regarding settler colonialism: "They steal your bread and give you a crumb of it. Then they demand you to thank them for their generosity. O their audacity!"

In an historic event that commenced in January 2024, South Africa, a nation that once experienced the oppression of an Apartheid regime, has taken a stand to assist another oppressed people, the Palestinians. South Africa has brought a case to the International Court of Justice (ICJ), accusing Israel of genocide. The allegations are grounded on the extensive devastation in Gaza, the ongoing and intentional targeting of civilian homes, hospitals, and individuals, and the detrimental effects on children which are indicative of genocidal intent.

Afterword

South Africa's submission of the genocide case against Israel to the ICJ has ignited rallies in Ramallah, West Bank, with Palestinians expressing their appreciation. South Africa's solidarity is rooted in a deep-seated alliance tracing back to Nelson Mandela and Yasser Arafat. As the ICJ hearings progressed, the claim carried considerable weight, influencing cultural, diplomatic, and historical aspects. For example, it challenges the core of Israel's national identity as a Jewish state, established in the wake of the Nazi-perpetrated Holocaust, and holds particular significance as it marks the first instance of a country accusing Israel of genocide in an international court.

As of January 2024, nearly all of the Gaza Strip's 2.3 million residents have lost their homes, enacting again the Nakba – or "Catastrophe" – of 1948 with its forced mass immigration of millions of displaced Palestinians into Lebanon and Jordan. The withholding of water, fuel, and electricity; the severe shortages of food that have resulted from the blockade of Gaza (in effect, the use of starvation as a weapon of war); the deliberate destruction of schools, hospitals and places of worship; have all led to a critical humanitarian crisis. If these are not considered crimes against humanity – as a form of apartheid, ethnic cleansing, or collective punishment – then what is? Again, this is why Kanafani stresses that "Palestine is a cause for every revolutionary, wherever he is ... a cause of the exploited and oppressed masses."

The true political artist does not merely document the events of the day but stands as an unbribable witness to the depths to which humankind has fallen. As a visionary, they also herald the new world to come, which is just out of sight. Such an artist is a reporter on the state of our soul, a sort of spirit-journalist. Oppression and injustice might be challenged through art, as Kanafani knew and Mahmoud Darwish articulated in a handful of words: "Poetry is an act of resistance." The artist as resistance figure, might be driven from their home – during the 1948 Palestine war, twelve-year-old Kanafani along with his family were forced out of their hometown – yet they continue to carry it in their hearts wherever they live. The intense shame the young Kanafani experienced as he witnessed the men of his family surrendering their weapons to become refugees also remained with him and fueled his righteously indignant art.

PALESTINE WAIL

Wherever refugees might attempt to start a new life, they must grapple with a sense of belonging, even homelessness. In a sense, refugees must always feel as if they were already somehow "posthumous," as though they are outliving themselves, having died to all that they once knew. The uprooted citizen continues to pine for what has been lost, experiencing an absolute and impossible love for "home," as they yearn for an ideal. Exiled, they wander the world like strangers, forever out-of-place. This is why artists must make a homeland of their art, dipping their pens and brushes into the ink of their aching heart, for both remembrance and inspiration. And when your home is burning, you feel the heat halfway across the world.

Nearly four years ago, on Valentine's Day, revered Palestinian poet Mourid Barghouti passed away, joining his beloved wife, novelist Radwa Ashour. At the age of seventy-six, Barghouti, a poet of lifelong exile, was four years older than the state of Israel at the time and wrote movingly about the twin sins of occupation and oppression. In his acclaimed autobiographical novel *I Saw Ramallah*, Barghouti describes returning to his beloved Palestine, for the first time in three decades, in these memorable words:

> The homeland does not leave the body until
>   the last moment, the moment of death.
> The fish,
> Even in the fisherman's net,
> Still carries
> The smell of the sea.

Publication Credits

With gratitude to the following editors, where these poems appear:

Open Letter to Israel, *Electronic Intifada*

Alternative Scenario, *Sojourners*

The Eclipse, *Phoebe Journal*

Peace, Lily
Blasphemous Praise, *Rowayat*

Why Care About Gaza,
Stranger in a Strange Land,
Overwhelming Emotion
Waking Nightmares
You Win, by Losing
During a Genocide
Gaza, Capital of Hurt, *Democracy in Exile*, a journal of Democracy for the Arab World Now (DAWN)

Purity,
Poems Sailing,
Hungering, *Charter for Compassion*

Palestinian Music,
Starving, *Wordpeace*

Fever Dream, *Lips Poetry* (Israel/Hebrew)

Columbia University, *Pangyrus*

Choices,
Hungering, *ArLiJo: Arlington Literary Journal*

For Israel, Palestine & the Human Family,
What to Say, First,
Resume,
Eros & Thanatos,
Walls, *WordCityLit*

Say Something
Control, *Lote Tree Press*

The Lightkeepers, *Fair Observer*

The Limits of Love, *American Scholar* (Read Me a Poem)

What Tragedy Teaches Us
Middle East Advice, *Tiferet Journal*

You, Again, sung by Israeli band *Hazelnuts* at a concert in Jerusalem

Lectio Divina, *Arabology*

Summary, *Escape Into Life*

For John, *Sufi Journal*

White, *Kosmos: Journal for Global Transformation*

Secrets, *Philosophy Now* magazine

Minister of Loneliness, *Spiritus Journal*

Garden Meditation, *Exterminating Angel Press*

Fine, Tuning, *Torch : University of Oxford*

I Get It, Now,
Re: Birth, *Poets Respond to the Pandemic: St. Michael's Arlington*

I Ran, *A Kaleidoscope of Stories:* Muslim Voices in Contemporary Poetry

Two Types of Kisses: *The Punch* magazine

Hunter and Hunted, *Tell Me More: NPR*

Acknowledgement

The shape of this book and its arc are thanks to multifaceted writer, poet, and scholar Mark S. Burrows, whom I'm fortunate to also call a friend. While I composed much of this collection in a semi-trance, emotionally overwhelmed, Mark helped to clarify its vision, trimming and putting poems into sections – a kind of musical, inner movement from outrage to anguished sorrow to measured hope.

Thanks, to him, *Palestine Wail* begins with my meditation on Hope and ends with Silence... In this progression, I felt that Mark was revealing me to myself, while amplifying the spiritual undercurrent throughout. As a subtle listener, and sympathetic spirit, he was able to overhear my longing, higher self, wishing to discern Divine will amid the madness and surrender to it.

I believe that in this time of great upheaval, Mark was heaven sent—more spiritual guide than mere editor. In the midst of the monstrous, murderous chaos, he reminded me time and again (sometimes, through 'my' own words) to not lose sight of the humanity of others, to remain humble and praise.

Thank you, Mark, for your sensitivity, knowingness and patience, over the nearly six-month period during which you worked, closely, with me, refining my "Wail". I and this book are better because of your fine guidance.

Yahia Lababidi is the author of eleven collections of poetry and prose. His aphorisms and poems have gone viral, are used in classrooms, religious services and have been featured at international film festivals.

Lababidi has also contributed to news, literary, and cultural institutions throughout the USA, Europe and the Middle East, including Oxford University, Pearson, the PBS NewsHour, NPR, HBO as well as ABC Radio.

His latest work includes a collection of his aphorisms on morality and mortality, *Quarantine Notes* (Fomite Press, 2023), *Desert Songs* (Rowayat, 2022), a bilingual, photographic account of mystical encounters in the desert, and *Learning to Pray* (Kelsay Books, 2021), a collection of spiritual reflections.

Titles of interest from Daraja Press

Mental Health and Human Rights in Palestine
Wasseem El Sarraj

This is a biography of the life of Dr Eyad El Sarraj, Gaza's pioneering psychiatrist and founder of the Gaza Community Mental Healthcare Programme, written by his son Wasseem. It is also a history of Palestine with a focus on Gaza. Eyad's life was intimately intertwined with Palestine's struggles so his choices and reactions reflected many of the major historical moments of the last 70 years.

ISBN 978-1-990263-37-8 • 132 pages • https://bityl.co/DSZO

Struggling to be seen: The travails of Palestinian cinema
Anandi Ramamurthy, Paul Kelemen

The book explores the challenges Palestinian filmmakers confront to develop a cinema that gives expression to the national narrative. The writers explore the political, economic and cultural factors that impact on Palestinian film production and the barriers encountered in profiling and screening Palestinian films.

ISBN 978-1-988832-80-7 • 84 pages • https://bit.ly/3tH9PW7

Claim No Easy Victories: The Legacy of Amilcar Cabral
Firoze Manji

Revolutionary, poet, liberation philosopher, and leader of the anticolonial independence movement of Guinea Bissau and Cape Verde, Amílcar Cabral's legacy stretches well beyond the shores of West Africa. In this unique collection of essays, radical thinkers from across Africa, the U.S., and internationally commemorate Cabral's life and legacy and his relevance to contemporary struggles.

ISBN 978-1-990263-64-4 • 490 pages

I See the Invisible
Nnimmo Bassey

This collection has a dose of meditative poems and others that reflect on the colonial and neoliberal foundations that permit willful disconnect from nature and allow rapacious extractivism. They also speak to the criminalization of environmental defenders and burdening of victims with survival struggles with no life boughs. These are poems that call for action.

ISBN 978-1-990263-89-7• 146 pages

Order from **darajapress.com**

Daraja Press

www.ingramcontent.com/pod-product-compliance
Lightning Source LLC
Chambersburg PA
CBHW070049100426
42734CB00040B/2884